# Disturbed One
## An Elder's Insightful Journey

David sa-see Spencer Sr.

Other Books by David sa-see Spencer Sr.
*The Poems of a Widower*
*Elder Abandonment*

Disturbed One
An Elder's Insightful Journey
All Rights Reserved.
Copyright © 2022 David sa-see Spencer Sr.
v1.0

This is a work of poeticized non-fiction. The opinions expressed in this manuscript are solely the opinions of the author and do not represent the opinions or thoughts of the publisher. The author has represented and warranted full ownership and/or legal right to publish all the materials in this book.

This book may not be reproduced, transmitted, or stored in whole or in part by any means, including graphic, electronic, or mechanical without the express written consent of the publisher except in the case of brief quotations embodied in critical articles and reviews.

Outskirts Press, Inc.
http://www.outskirtspress.com

ISBN: 978-1-9772-5316-3

Cover Photo © 2022 David D. Spencer Sr.

Outskirts Press and the "OP" logo are trademarks belonging to Outskirts Press, Inc.

PRINTED IN THE UNITED STATES OF AMERICA

Dedicated to
Katherine Mary Campbell

Water blisters spread
In the forest's wet
Underbrush. Infested
With mountain dew.

Sticky raindrops
Crash steadily
On the bald head.
Streaking in the rain.

The winter night
Mist-droplets spattered
On the elder's
Stuck out tongue.
A gargling jubilee.

The zealous
Elder waltzed
With the swirling
Feathery snowflakes.
The bliss flows beyond the mind!

The heavenly
Rain attempted
To whitewash
The red tongue.
The uninterested elder
Still yawned.
Ah-oh-hoo.

The unmerciful
White caps kidnapped
The zapped raindrops.
A Puget Sound lightning
Storm on a yowling rampage.

The liberated souls
Pop up and down.
Sightlessly, they hurl themselves
In the bugling darkness.
Freedom celebration!

The squealing elder's
Anemic blood drained
By the thirsty stalkers.
Damn prickly mosquitoes.

The breathless
Shadows mummified
The forgotten elder.
Ancestors crept nearby with
Their spiritual alertness.

The dwarfish
Shadows shrug off
Their own afterlife.
They shimmy away from
The engulfing morning sun.

The wooden wind
Chimes swatted repeatedly
By the malicious wind.
Godawful thuds echoed back.

The ancestor's chants
Soar with the westerly wind.
The emptiness ripped open
By their rebirth shrieks.

The winter fog
Exhumed the body
Of the lifeless elder.
The crusty diehard floats
Into the dark vastness.

The stricken
Elder was exhausted
By the dyeing heart scans.
They revealed the gummy
Blood clots.

The elder unperturbed
As the droopy fat protects
The six-pack tummy.
Unashamed secret.

The endless heart
Murmurs silently as it
Tucks in the rooted blood clots.
The red-eyed elder still struts.

Hospital ER test-testy
Flashes a risky-risk pumper.
Trauma trickster. 01

Rapid detonating
Heartbeats implode
In the fidgety elder.
The blissful soul gnaws
The edges of the raw heart.

A short-winded
Elder had two-stepped
To the tweaky heartbeat.
Teetering
Left foot____
____Right foot
Left foot____
____Right foot

Peaked heart pangs
Were flatten by the agonizing
sighs of the panting elder.
The scarred heart was reset.

The elder's mind
Wasn't at all altered
By the weird intimacy.
Crazed couple embraced and
Asked nothing from each other.

The westerly rain rams
Against the fevered elder.
The rain pecks the hollow-man and
Dams his mute soul.

Finally, the elder
Accepts being the faceless man,
The blurred ancient one.
He is a freethinking grunter now.
The skinned elder still exists.

Elder gobbles a tart
Onion like a ripe apple.
Oh, mouthy stench explodes!

Are you deranged
Because that beauty
Made eye to eye contact
With me? Oh, I'm not ashamed,
the aged flirter forgives you.

Ho, I briefly realize
The tribal healing chants
Are fluttering around me.
Resurrecting excitement within me.

Elder's own loud guttural
Chant flows through
The knotted forest shadows.
His echo howls back.

His reclusive spirit
Devoured the elder's
Own anguishing chant.
The elder choked
On his own nothingness.

With each elder's breath
His chant was tongue-tied.
An unending ritual.

An elder's chant
Bellows with deafening,
"Ooh-ho-s, ooh-ho-s"
Jabbing the inflated silence.

The drumming elder
Circles the slim-like
Crawlers. The eye-slit snakes
Hiss at each boom-boom.

The tipsy soul
Fades in and out
From nothingness.
The elder impulsively
Chant hums in the suicidal abyss.

Who is it here?
Who invades in my mind?
Oh, my own dead brother. 02

Her ridiculous vivid
War-painted face tickles
The wobbly elder.
His joyful giggles hidden.

Heard the sti'talh whistle
Through the forest tree tops.
The gusting Forces raged
And hurled broken branches
Downward. Sti'talh swirled.

The knuckled elder's
mindfulness trickling
The guarded throaty moans.
Oh, flirtation thorny chaos.

Daily the elder
Gawked at a stark
Thistly face in the mirror.
Cannibalistic white whiskers.

The elder thrashed
By low unhuman yearns.
The savage Changer,
Blubbering suicidal thoughts.

Elder ignorant
Of his own hoarding
Addiction. Enshrines
His own decaying memories.

The edges of elder's
Insights hardened daily.
No expectations nightly
Except the infant-like drooling.

Awe – delirious elder
Awakens guiltless with
Snippets of deceitful lust.

The elder obsessed
With the life riddles
Of resurrected ancestors.
Searched for his own mystique.

The renegading
Elder unveils his own belief.
The Mother Earth and the freckled
Goddess are tensed sisters.

Very real slobber
Dripped from the elder's
Quivering red lips.
Oh, strawberries and cake!

Just babbling about and
Determined to sound alive.
Loosen the suicidal grip
As there is no climax today.
Fearless eyes rekindled.

Elder's mindfulness
Of own slow sissified swagger.
Gurgling, 'oh-ho-ooh.'
Hurling the suicidal woes
Out of the presence.

The muted wisdom rehashed
By this gaping old carcass.
Who would care to listen?
Elder yields to the ticking void.

The elder's reflection
Of his whimsical double.
The double hacks the old brain
And laps up the ceremonial blood.
Hush-hush wanton rebirth.

The self-awareness had
A sense of being so invincible.
The mishmash of inaudible joy.
Yet recognized the senile fear.

The heinous tantrums
Have dismembered the past.
The bawling elder cracks
Open the hollow skull.

Do fugitive souls still
Recall their first bleating
Birth cries? Elder gags and
Gags on his own rebirth cry.

Squinting elder so intent
For the simple burial.
Deathless over deathless
Was his childlike belief.

Disturbed elder zoned out
In his own eerie seclusion.
He giggled and pranced
Along as the Life-Changer.

Elder sprawled under
The faded holey-blanket.
The widower's skull
Slammed from the stabbing wails.

Widower's tears for a dead love
Burdened his impotent soul.
Elder's own innocence had been
Muzzled first then amputated.

The tattered exclusion
Of the elderly wisdom
Favors his own indifference.

Shivering elder's
Breath had steamed
The pale sky reddish,
The bloody Changer!

The bleak moon's
Beams raked deep
Into the ditch's bowels.
Digested a bloody red dress.

Elder's muzzled life worms
Out from his wordless boredom.
Oh joy! A lip popper. Oh joy!

Blissfully, his mouth
Mangled the animal cookies.
A smacking savage.

The mouth twanging with
Loud smacking, 'Yummy,
Yummy for the tummy!'
The cookie crumbs explode.

Stoic soul alarmed
As the elder's teeth
Blasted outward.
Hysterical laughter.

Jilted elder's suicidal
Dreams were scraped
Out of the grub-like head.
The dreams of temptation
Are just smoldering now.

Easygoing elder
Hobbled below
The burial mounds.
Yet, the inner child
Boogied and boogied.

Silliness topples
Elder's afterlife thoughts.
Tucked under pristine dirt
And away from the woe-be-gones.
Feels the blooming flowers.

Exceeding the moment
Of an innocent gawking.
Chocolate cake awaits.

Lumbering elder looked
At a pitted river rock.
The weight of its nothingness
Was heavy on the recluse.
Yet, it tapped his soul.

The dark moon
Unbleached the snow.
The pulsing darkness
Had ravished the mind.
The soul peeled itself off
With each falling breath.

Unconsciously,
The daffy elder tramples
On the dainty white daisies,
A cocky beauty crusher.

The tall grass flogged
The underbelly of the dog.
Its paws thumped back.

Nestled in dying bitterness
Among the sprouting shadows.
The droopy eyed elder just
Yearned for a single touch.

The spraying wet snow
Leeched my ghostly breath.
It clung to my thick skull and
I sunk into its hungry abyss.
Yet, I whispered, "Fly."

Clinging winter fog
Crept down the feeble elder
Who was frozen dead silent.
Temptation of emptiness.

The gorging pain had
Clawed the cynical mind
And kept the bald elder mute.
Cleansed the heartache wounds.

This scarred elder
Stood in the final
Abandonment. Scalded
Raw by the lively smirks of the youth.
Sssh, sssh aging ah-coming,
Ah-coming for the youth.
Sssh, sssh.

Again, the drowsy
Elder drools nightly
With the invading shadows.
Flawless bliss in staying alive.

The winged elder
Soars out of the unconscious abyss.
He whispers chants to own
Caressing ancestors. Oh whooie!

Isn't self-reliance
A festering virtuous trait?
Elder resigned to be the walking-dead.
His gay soul was swoop looping.

What finicky testament
Does a banished elder have?
The wooing suicide could
Be a brattish folly.

Oh, mutilating aging
A callous form of ghoulish torture.
Skinless soul manages to
Unmuzzle the blooming joy.

Oh, my playful mind
Witnessed the crawling grass.
Oh! It's the disturbed one, snake.
The serpent hissed and recoiled
On the grass tentacles.

Lone coyote howls
At the ballooning twilight sky.
Oh gosh, I'm not alone here.
Childishly, I howl too.
Howling the barbed evil away.

Mute elder pretends
His throbbing ailments are ok.
Entrusts solitude.

## Subscript 01

ER trip revealed two issues: a minor damage to heart tissue and restricted blood in the heart - additional detail heart scan was scheduled - no worry - all seems well with I....

## *Subscript 02*

Whenever I dreamt of my older brother Butch that passed away back in 1974. We always communicated through telepathy – spiritual brothers.

## *Subscript 03*

Lushootseed word sti'alh means mystical forest person. Each modern tribal generation has lost the myth knowledge of our sti'talh people. Sti'alh are alive when we hear and believe in them, The Lushootseed Language is still spoken by tribal indigenous people within the Puget Sound of Washington State.

## *Subscript 04*

Poem to honor our Murdered and Missing Indigenous Women.... Poem insight.... The Moon Goddess continuously probes the ground. She sinks deeply into the mouth of Mother Earth and finds only a bloody red dress. Moon Goddess lifts our murdered Sister's tribal Spirit. Mother Earth gathers in and cleanses our Indigenous Sister.

About the author....

David sa-see Spencer Sr. is the author of four poetry chapbooks and an autobiography of his life up to the age of 19. He was raised by his tribal grandparents on the Tulalip Indian Reservation, Tulalip, Washington. He is 85 years old and a tribal elder enrolled in The Tulalip Tribes.

David retired from the General Telephone Company, Everett, Washington after thirty years of employment.

He attended the Everett Community College, Everett, Washington and the University of Washington, Seattle, Washington. David studied poetry from Nelson Bentley, a poet and English Professor at the University of Washington.

The chapbook cover's photograph is a cement head handmade by David Spencer Sr. He is a visual artist who has created linocut block prints, paintings, dichro glass fusing of pendants, wood carvings, small cement sculptures and short videos of reading his own poetry and chanting his own tribal Lushootseed songs.

CPSIA information can be obtained
at www.ICGtesting.com
Printed in the USA
BVHW032159160422
634531BV00011B/127